Published in 2023 by Orange Mosquito
An Imprint of Welbeck Children's Limited
part of Welbeck Publishing Group.
Based in London and Sydney.
www.welbeckpublishing.com

In collaboration with Mosquito Books Barcelona S.L.

© Mosquito Books Barcelona, SL 2022
Text © Soledad Romero Mariño 2022
Illustration © Montse Galbany 2022
Translation: Maria White
Publisher: Margaux Durigon
Production: Jess Brisley

ISBN: 9781914519703
eISBN: 9781914519710

Printed in India
10 9 8 7 6 5 4 3 2 1

FSC
www.fsc.org
MIX
Paper from
responsible sources
FSC® C010615

Soledad Romero Mariño • Montse Galbany

Disgustingly Delicious

The surprising, weird and wonderful food of the word

ORANGE
M·O·S·Q·U·I·T·O

6 Jellied eels
ENGLAND

12 Stinky herrings
SWEDEN

7 Blood soup
GERMANY

9 Duck liver pâté
FRANCE

14 Fresh milk and blood shake
KENYA AND TANZANIA

13 Hairy caterpillars
SOUTH AFRICA

Stinky tofu
TAIWAN

17

16 Fried tarantula
CAMBODIA

15 Poop coffee
INDONESIA

19 Giant tuna eyeballs
JAPAN

18 Wriggling live octopus
JAPAN AND SOUTH KOREA

"Disgust is always subjective. It depends on where you were brought up. It is as if we are brainwashed from a young age about what is disgusting and what is not."
Andreas Ahrens – Director of The Disgusting Food Museum (Sweden)

Surströmming

Frog shake

An Inca breakfast

In the market in Lima, the locals and a few intrepid tourists line up for a breakfast of the popular and vitamin-filled frog juice that they prepare there.

The outdoor stalls are small and a little run down and bright posters advertise the benefits of their juices.

Egg

Honey

Brewer's yeast

Cereals

Pollen

Aloe vera

Maca

Consumers claim they have energy all day thanks to the juice, and that it even overcomes all kinds of health problems. According to them, the juice possesses healing and aphrodisiac properties.

Each stall keeps their frogs in large glass tanks while they wait for the client to order their juice at the counter.

At that point, the frog is put it into a blender with the rest of the ingredients: eggs, maca (a vegetable root from the Andes), cereals, pollen, aloe vera, brewer's yeast, honey... Every stall has its own recipe, but all of the combinations are made to be healthy and nutritious.

The main and most important ingredient is brought alive from Lake Titicaca.

PERU

Lima

Lake Titicaca

It is delicious!

This mixture is a powerful breakfast from the Andes. A preparation based on centuries of tradition, ever since the Incas first drank it.

Even so, it has been criticized for leaving this species of frog in danger of extinction.

Ant Larvae

Escamoles

Although it might sound disgusting to most of the world to eat ant larvae, in Mexico escamoles are one of the most exclusive and delicious dishes you could try.

This dish, also known as "Mexican caviar," is a delicacy that is unbelievably expensive because it is very complicated to collect the larvae of this gigantic species of ant.

They are only served in luxury restaurants.

There are three big problems for those who collect these larvae:

They can only be collected once a year; as ants just reproduce during the months of March and April.

The ants hide their nests several yards deep. The only method the collector has of finding the ant nests is to follow a line of ants zigzagging through the jungle. Once the nest is located, they dig a 10-foot pit to access it.

The ants are aggressive, and their bites are very painful. The collector is exposed to attack by ferocious ants that are legitimately protecting the eggs in their colony.

Oww! They are biting me!

Once they have managed to extract the larvae from the nest, the collectors wash them in water to remove the earth. It is a very delicate process as one wrong move could break the larvae's thin outer layer.

Cooking them does not require many ingredients. To maintain the exotic and delicate flavor of the larvae, simply stir-fry them in a pan with a little butter, onion, and some aromatic spices. There are many recipes, each chef has their own way of preparing this exotic and traditional dish.

Escamoles are a delicacy that have more than a thousand years of history. The women of Mesoamerican people cooked them long before the Spanish conquistadors arrived. They were already an essential part of their diet, highly appreciated for their delicious flavor and their extraordinary nutritional value: escamoles have four times more protein than the best meat.

When the Spanish conquistadors arrived in these lands, they celebrated this food above all the other delicacies that this wonderful and fertile land had to offer.

Mesoamerican women

CANADA

UNITED
STATES

3
Fried Testicles

Rocky Mountain oysters

Rocky Mountain oysters are the fried testicles of a bull, sheep, buffalo or wild boar.

When the Spanish conquistadors arrived in these lands, they celebrated this food above all the other delicacies that this wonderful and fertile land had to offer.

They began to cook and eat testicles to avoid wasting the meat when they castrated (removed the testicles of) their animals.

Castrating their animals meant they could tame them, fatten them up, and control the number of livestock.

There are many ways to prepare this traditional and peculiar delicacy. The first step is to peel the testicles, inside they are white and are shaped like an oyster. This is where the name of the dish comes from.

The next step is to soak them. They can be soaked in salted water, in water, and vinegar; some even do it in beer or milk. Then they are cut into slices and coated in flour, egg, salt, and pepper—ready to fry in lots of vegetable oil.

The result is a crunchy and tasty apéritif, ideal with a spicy sauce.

How incredible! This bull is huge!

This is a typical delicacy of ranch festivities which are usually celebrated in the spring.

Some believe that you can learn to enjoy this dish by eating it often. It is what they call an acquired taste. Even so, there are many tourists who ask for the popular Rocky Mountain oysters when they go to a traditional restaurant in the United States or when they take part in traditional festivities.

Fermented Birds

Kiviak

In the north of Greenland the Inuit have succeeded in surviving low temperatures and thousands of miles of ice for hundreds of years.

GREENLAND

Nuuk

The Inuit are nomadic. For centuries, they traveled across the Arctic hunting prey: bears, whales, seals, fish, and birds; they use every part of the body to feed and protect themselves from the cold.

In the months when the hunting is good, the Inuit prepare a traditional, centuries-old, putrid dish which has allowed them to survive: *kiviak*.

The recipe is simple, although the dish is only suitable for the strongest stomachs.

Wow!

First, they place 500 dead auks (a kind of marine bird) inside a completely gutted seal. The birds are left whole: with feathers, beaks, and legs.

Once they have filled the seal, they sew it up, seal it with fat and flatten it with rocks. In this way, they make sure there is no air left inside and flies can't get in. **Air would make the meat decompose and maggots would destroy the product.**

The birds remain inside the seal for seven months, completely insulated from the outside world. Once this time has passed, the seal can be opened and the birds, which have fermented inside it, can be eaten.

Auk

Fermented birds in a seal skin

In the past, the seal would be opened when food was scarce. It was a way of conserving food. These days, this dish is reserved for special occasions: birthdays, weddings, Christmas, or other big celebrations.

Once the seal is open, the birds are taken out; the smell is terrible but the fermented birds are ready to eat. They require no other preparation, except plucking the bird's feathers, to access the meat. The bird can be eaten on its own or with a garnish.

In Greenland, this dish is considered a very exclusive and expensive delicacy.

Cured Shark

Hákarl

Many consider Hákarl one of the most disgusting foods in the world, however in Iceland, it is considered a deliciously smelly Viking delicacy.

Glug, glug, glug!

3.2 ft

Proportion of actual size of Anna to the Greenland shark.

In Iceland, traditions are very important. It is a place which is very proud of its history and its Viking ancestors who, when they conquered the island centuries ago, made the Greenland shark their primary source of food.

The Greenland shark was abundant in the icy waters of the North Atlantic, but its flesh was poisonous to human beings. However, in those times, there was not much else to eat so the ingenious Vikings created a technique to make the shark's meat edible.

The key to the recipe is eliminating the poison the shark contains: trimethylamine oxide and ureic acid (a component found in urine).

It is a long, slow production process that begins with gutting the almost 26-foot-long shark. Once clean, it is put in a pit and covered with stones, sand, and gravel.

The strong smell of the shark forced the Vikings to bury the animal in a distant place.

The pressure from the rocks causes the animal's poisonous fluid to be filtered out so the meat ferments properly. After 6-12 weeks, the shark is ready to be dug up.

The last step is drying. For this, the shark is hung up in pieces in a dark, well-ventilated place for three to four months. When the animal's skin has dried and is brown in color, it is ready to be skinned

ICELAND
Reykjavik

ATLANTIC OCEAN

A

B

C

D

and cut into dice-sized cubes. The smell the shark gives off is acidic and rancid—it reminds you of a mixture of fermented cheese and ammonia.

Only locals seem to be capable of enjoying this rancid delicacy. Foreigners mostly hold their noses when they put a piece of shark in their mouth, to avoid the overwhelming stench. Once getting past the putrid smell, they are faced with—perhaps—the most rancid and gut-wrenching taste on planet Earth.

To make eating this snack easier, it is usually served with a typical Icelandic spirit which helps cleanse the palette.

Jellied Eels

Jellied eels

Jellied eels were a creation of the working class who lived in the English capital of London during the industrial revolution.

In the kitchens of the poorest neighborhoods, they began to cook the unsavory eels found living in the river that crossed through London: the Thames.

The river Thames

Poverty and hunger turned a greasy food into a superfood; preparing workers to face long, hard days in the factories. It turned out to be an excellent product that was close at hand, cheap, and nutritious.

ENGLAND

London

To make this dish, first the dead eels are cut into slices. Then they are cooked for an hour in water with vinegar, lemon juice, herbs, and spices.

When the eels are done, they are left to cool in the stock so that it forms a tasty jelly.

Jellied eels are served cold with a strong, spicy vinegar sauce.

There are few things more strange, slimy, and British than this dish; but it is very fashionable these days and it is on the menu in traditional pubs and cafes in London. It is also sold in jars in supermarkets in the country.

JELLIED EELS

Blood Soup

Schwarzsauer

Duck offal

Blood from a slaughter

Bay leaf

Cinnamon

Pepper

Many religions and cultures prohibit the use of blood as food. They consider it disgusting and connected to evil. Yet blood is inevitably the main by-product of any slaughter and a very healthy nutrient. This is why a lot of cultures have introduced this valuable substance into their cuisine.

Foods that use blood have traveled throughout all the continents of the planet. It is surprising the number of recipes that offer this succulent delicacy, so strongly linked to vampire stories.

In the north of Germany, they use pig blood to make a traditional Schwarzsauer soup.

GERMANY

Water

Vinegar

Sugar

Salt

Onion

Garlic

Dried fruit

The soup is a dish that combines blood with many other ingredients, including duck offal (edible organs). The concoction is boiled in a large pot and flavored with vinegar, spices, sugar, onion, and dried fruit.

The result is a soup served hot to help combat the cold. This recipe is usually produced in large quantities. It is customary to store the soup in glass jars.

Changes in taste in the German population, increasingly moving toward vegetarian foods, have made this dish lose popularity and little by little it has become a delicacy connected to old traditions.

Snails

Escargots de Bourgogne

The snails spend several days in a tub without food. The aim is for them to release saliva and excrement before being washed and scrubbed with salted water or water with vinegar.

Burgundy
FRANCE

Chicken stock

Butter

Garlic

Parsley

Once clean, the snails are put in a cooking pot with boiling water for a moment. Now the snails can be extracted from their shells and their guts removed.

The snails are cooked in a tasty chicken stock. Then they are put back in their shells, together with a sauce made from butter, garlic, and parsley.

The snails are arranged, facing up, on a special plate with hollows to prevent the shell from turning over.

A couple of minutes in the oven is enough for the tasty butter to flood and fill the shell with its flavor. Then they are ready to eat.

Burgundy snails are a typical French dish. In general, they are served as a starter in restaurants.

LET'S PROTECT THEIR HABITAT!

NO TO PESTICIDES

The relentless disappearance of the snail's natural habitat and the use of pesticides seriously threatens their population so, since 1970, French edible snails are a protected species.

The skill of the dinner guest is important to enjoy the snails. You must use a snail fork to extract it from the shell which you hold with tongs. The snails are usually eaten with bread.

Their consumption began in the French region of Burgundy, but during the second half of the nineteenth century their fame spread, and they became fashionable in all of France.

This is their actual size.

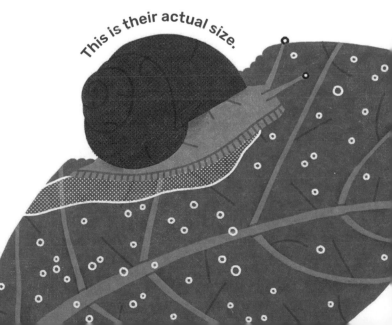

Duck Liver Pâté

Foie gras

Ducks, geese, and other migratory birds store vast quantities of fat in their livers.

This fat is the energy reserve that allows them to fly enormous distances around the world.

For thousand of years, this type of bird has taken refuge from the cold on the pleasant banks of the Nile, in Egypt.

This is when the people of Ancient Egypt discovered the exquisite taste hidden inside the birds' fatty livers (foie gras).

Very cleverly, Egyptian farmers began to fatten their domestic geese in a bid to recreate the delicious taste of the fatty liver of these wild birds.

Duck

Domestic goose

Liver

The process was a success, and a thousand-year-old delicacy was born on those banks that soon conquered the whole Mediterranean.

The process of fattening the liver of these birds is cruel.

They are force-fed a fatty corn-based substance. Once the liver has reached the desired size, the nerves are removed and it is left to soak in cold water and ice; then the liver is ready to be cooked.

Foie gras is considered by some to be a top ingredient that takes any recipe to another level. Foie gras can be spread on a simple piece of bread, changing it into a delicacy.

Despite the controversial method of producing foie gras, it continues to be considered a luxury ingredient in many countries and reserved for major celebrations.

Today, France is the main producer of foie gras in the world, although its sale is prohibited in more than 15 countries because it is considered a forced food, a type of cruelty to animals

Stewed Cow's Intestines

Callos

The less important parts of a slaughtered animal are known as offal. These remnants go into an enormous sack, including: intestines, testicles, ears, eyes, brains, hearts, feet, tongue.

Although many cuisines shy away from offal, in the Castile region in Spain, there is a long tradition of cooking with these highly valued ingredients.

Callos is a medley made with tripe (stomach lining) and intestines, and is one of the most typical and famous Spanish dishes using offal.

It was created in the taverns of the capital, Madrid, during medieval times; when people were dying of hunger and necessity created this peculiar yet tasty stew.

Callos is prepared with the intestines and other offal from a cow. In olden days, people left the offal to soak for 24 hours to clean it. These days, they buy it already cleaned at the butchers.

CASA MARÍA

18

CALLOS
A LA
MADRILEÑA

VERMOUTH
ON TAP

To cook the stew, intestines are put in a large cooking pot with the rest of the ingredients: beef stock, tomato sauce, garlic, and a lot of local spices (paprika, cloves, bay leaf, nutmeg, thyme, chili pepper, and rosemary).

Madrid

SPAIN

Pimentón

The cooking process takes a while.

Little by little, the gelatin from the offal dissolves and combines with the aromatic spices; bringing together the various flavors. The stew will be ready in a few hours but the next day its flavor is much richer (as is the case with a lot of stews).

Callos are served in a clay pot layered with ham and slices of chorizo and black pudding. Bread is essential to mop up the sauce.

The stew is eaten hot and ideally when the weather is cold. But callos is also cooked in the summer; It is a snack that can still be eaten in the typical bars and restaurants of Madrid.

Maggot Cheese

Casu marzu

The exquisite and sought-after flavor of this cheese is the result of the maggots that live, eat, and excrete inside it.
Dinner guests cut a slice of the creamy cheese, full of maggots, and spread it on bread. Then they put it in their mouths and press it against their palate—to enjoy the full taste of this peculiar and highly valued cheese.

ITALY

Sardinia

The maggots can jump up to 6 inches. There have been cases where a maggot has jumped under the eyelid of a dinner guest. So you better watch out!

This cheese, made from sheep's milk and fly larvae, is originally from a region in Sardinia. When they prepare the cheese, they leave it next to an open window so that flies, attracted by its creamy smell, pierce the cheese and leave their eggs inside.

During the fermentation, the hatched larvae live comfortably for several weeks, feeding on the cheese, only to finally be devoured with it.

The work of the larvae makes the cheese creamy with a strong spicy taste. But you should know that enjoying this delicacy can have a few secondary effects: including stomach pain.

The sale of this cheese is prohibited in Italy. However, families on this Italian island have been preparing this peculiar dish for many decades and are eager to carry on the tradition.

Rotten cheese with live maggots

Stinky Herrings

Surströmming

SWEDEN

Baltic
Sea

The stinkiest fermented herring in the world comes in a can and is the work of the Swedes.

Surst...

It is recommended that the can is opened outside because of the terrible smell of rotting fish. The fish is opened along the middle to clean out the guts, roe, and bones. Then they smash them with a fork and break them up into small pieces. It is usually eaten in a sandwich of soft, thin bread spread with butter. Diced onion and sliced boiled potatoes are added. As a final touch, add a little sour cream

The herrings used for surströmming are caught in spring (between April and May). They are stored whole and raw for one or two months in barrels where they begin their foul-smelling process of fermentation. Then they are canned. In six months, the fermentation process will have allowed the fish to reach their "extraordinary" acidic and rotten flavor. It is usual to see the cans inflate because of the potent gases generated during fermentation

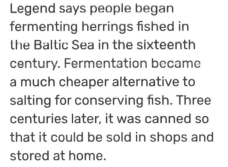

Legend says people began fermenting herrings fished in the Baltic Sea in the sixteenth century. Fermentation became a much cheaper alternative to salting for conserving fish. Three centuries later, it was canned so that it could be sold in shops and stored at home.

Surströmming is a Swedish delicacy that has divided the population. There is no middle ground: it is either considered delicious or disgusting.

Hairy Caterpillars
Madora

13

AFRICA

Namibia
Botswana
South Africa
Zimbabwe

Mopane
tree

Madora
caterpillar

Emperor moth

The caterpillars of the emperor moth are very disturbing hairy creatures that at first sight look quite revolting. But in fact, they are edible and have fed millions of people for centuries.

Madora caterpillars primarily feed on the leaves of the mopane tree, one of the few trees that can resist the scorching climate of Southern Africa. For centuries, the villagers of the region have been collecting these caterpillars to eat and to sell.

However, in the last 50 years, several companies have tried to exploit this community resource.

They organize large groups of collectors who gather the caterpillars to process and can them later. The caterpillar business is very profitable and makes millions of dollars per year.

When the locals catch the spiny caterpillar, they make a hole in the tail to squeeze and gut it—in the same way they would squeeze a tube of toothpaste.

Once gutted, the caterpillars are cleaned in water, then boiled and dried in the sun. It is also common to smoke them to give them additional flavor.

The caterpillars are eaten dried with an apéritif; they are quite tasteless but are crunchy. They can also be rehydrated to cook with fruit; served fried; or salted with a handful of onions, tomato, and spices. This combination is usually accompanied by pasta made from a white cornmeal flour called sadza.

MOPANE WORMS

MOPANE WORMS

MOPANE WORMS

$3.40

How crazy! They are enormous!

CRUNCH!

Sadza

Fresh Milk and Blood Shake

Maasai drink

The Maasai are a tribe of cattle farmers that live in Kenya and Tanzania. Their lives are one long journey in search of green pastures for their herds.

For the tribe, cows and everything related to the herd is sacred. They worship the land, pasture, water, and all sources of sustenance

The arrows they use have a wooden head.

KENYA
Nairobi

TANZANIA
Dodoma

Most of their foods come from the animals they care for, and the most powerful ancestral delicacy is a shake made from milk and fresh blood.

The most impressive thing about this concoction is that the blood is consumed directly from the neck of a live cow!

To obtain the blood without it coagulating, they put a tourniquet around the neck of the cow and push an arrow into the jugular (on the skin hanging around the neck).

With great precision, they collect the blood in a gourd where it is mixed with fresh milk.

The arrows they use have a wooden head that they sharpen with the intention of cutting and not mortally wounding the cow.

The cow stops bleeding and the wound closes quickly. They beat the mixture hard and drink it, passing the gourd around from one to another.

This ceremony has been passed down through the generations and can be repeated every month. The delicacy is reserved for special occasions or for those who are weak. The Maasai believe this drink reinforces their immune system.

Poop Coffee

Kopi luwak

INDONESIA

Although kopi luwak is the most expensive coffee in the world, many believe it is totally disgusting because it is prepared with beans pooped by a civet.

The civet is a small Indonesian marsupial, not much bigger than a cat. It lives among coffee bushes and feeds on its fruit.

To collect them, the villagers retrieve the beans by hand from the civet's poop. Then they wash them. And finally, they lightly toast them so as not to destroy their sweet flavor. Now the beans can be ground and prepared like traditional coffee.

The curious thing is that this little animal digests the pulp of the fruit and poops the bean. In addition, its sophisticated digestive system dissolves the proteins that make coffee bitter. Coffee prepared with these pooped beans has a smooth and exquisite caramel flavor.

When and who began collecting coffee beans from poop?

History dates it to the beginnings of the eighteenth century, during the time when Dutch colonists occupied Indonesia.

The colonists forced the villagers to cultivate coffee, but all the coffee harvested was sent to the Netherlands. Locals were forbidden from consuming the fruit of the fields they worked in.

For that reason, when they saw the beans among the civet poop, they did not hesitate to collect and use them. What a discovery! Without planning to, they had in their hands the most delicious coffee in the world.

Kopi luwak is a coffee for drinking on its own without sugar. This is the only way to taste its unique caramel flavor.

The traditional production of this coffee and its extraordinary flavor has turned this variety into a luxury reserved for wealthy people. There are very few cafés in the world that serve it as it is so expensive.

$$$

Fried Tarantula

Cambodian snack

In Cambodia, locals would die for a good fried tarantula. Among the great selection of insects available, it is a highly desired appetizer and also the most expensive.

The price is ridiculous compared to the cost of grasshoppers or cockroaches. And it has nothing to do with the danger involved in catching these wild spiders, compared to breeding other insects.

Salesmen sell them on the streets where cars and buses full of tourists make a customary stop to try this exotic snack.

Most tourists only try to eat the legs, which are very crunchy and salty, but locals assure them that the most delicious part of the tarantula is the white meat of the abdomen.

THAILAND

CAMBODIA

Phnom Penh

Salt Sugar Garlic Oil

The tarantulas eaten in Cambodia are the size of the palm of an average adult's hand. They are bred in the forests to the north, near the border with Thailand. Spider hunters bring their catch from there to the food stalls in towns.

They are kept in the stalls piled up in buckets for cooking throughout the day.

The spiders are fried in lots of oil with a little crushed garlic until the legs are crunchy. Then they are covered in sugar and salt.

This is their actual size.

Cambodians have long hunted spiders for food and medicine. However, during the '70s, tarantulas became a principal source of food for Cambodians.

Cambodia went through a horrific famine caused by a heartless government. The country had nothing to eat and, in desperation, tarantulas became an exotic food that saved them.

Stinky Tofu

Chòudòufu

The foul-smelling aroma of this type of tofu is a cross between rotten trash and smelly feet. This popular delicacy is like an assault on the senses but, according to experts, it is one of those delicacies where the more it smells—the more delicious it is.

It can be enjoyed in street markets and some restaurants. It is an experience to feel the soft white curd in the mouth and its all-conquering whiff in the nostrils.

Taipei

TAIWAN

Soya plant

Soya seeds

Tofu

Tofu is made from the seeds of the soya plant. It is also known as soya curd.

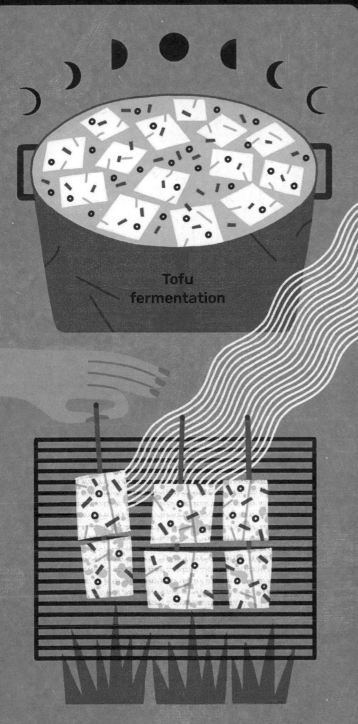

Tofu
fermentation

The secret to the smell is in the
fermentation that happens when the
tofu is marinated for several months in a
kind of stock made from fermented milk,
vegetables, meat, and herbs. Each cook
jealously guards their personal recipe.

The foul-smelling tofu can be eaten cold,
steamed, put on the grill, added to soup, stewed,
or fried. It is usually accompanied by spicy sauces
and all kinds of garnish.

**Some legends say that stinky tofu was the
accidental creation of a traveling salesman
in ancient China.**

The story says that one day the salesman was left
with a large quantity of unsold tofu. Not wanting
to throw it away, he cut it up into small pieces
and emptied it into a jar with stock. But he was
distracted and completely forgot about it.

After several days, the salesman opened the jar
and found that the tofu was green and stinky.
However, he tried the decayed tofu and found
that it was surprisingly delicious.

After that, he began selling it from his stall.
Day by day, it grew in popularity until he
succeeded in serving it at the imperial palace
of the Qing dynasty.

Wriggling Live Octopus

Sannakji

This dish consists of cutting live octopus into pieces, covering them with sesame oil, and serving immediately.

This dish is famous throughout the world for the surprising (and terrifying) spectacle it brings to the table.

In a restaurant, the ceremony begins when the client selects an octopus from the fish tank.

The experienced chef takes it out and begins gutting and cutting up the animal (without killing it) so that it is served at the table wriggling.

The diced animal wriggles on the plate until the dinner guest traps it with chop sticks and puts it in his mouth.

Sesame oil

It is important that all the pieces of octopus are well covered in oil so that the suckers on the tentacles, which still retain their strength, do not stick to the palate or tongue. It is also extremely important to chew well.

Fans of this dish enjoy the feeling of the octopus's movement in the mouth as much as the flavor of fresh meat.

Stories suggest that six people die each year from choking on this lively delicacy. .

The consumption of live animals is a traditional custom in many eastern and southeast Asian cultures.

In Japan, this type of cuisine is called *ikizukuri* (prepared live). Although many disapprove of it and laws against animal cruelty prohibit it, there are still animals (like prawns, lobster, and other types of fish) that are subjected to this horrible preparation.

The story says that Kendo fighters, the Japanese fencers, ate sannakji to gain strength and the courage necessary to fight.

Giant Tuna Eyeballs

The popular "delicacy"

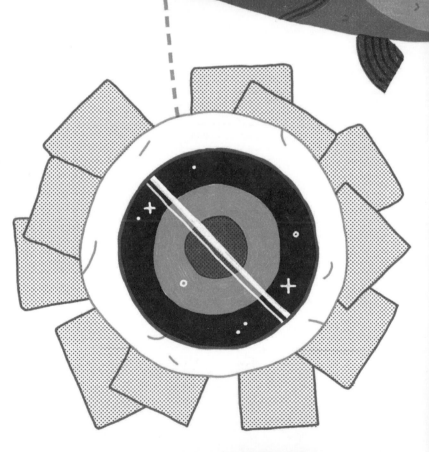

Tuna eyeballs are an impressive size and have quite a special taste. The bravest eat them raw, cut into pieces and served with a shot of Sake (a very strong Japanese spirit). But the healthiest and most nutritious option is to eat them when cooked.

The Japanese can buy tuna eyeballs in any supermarket. It is astonishing to see the eyeballs, almost as big as tennis balls, sitting on ice trays. In Japan, people often cook them for a special dinner.

These delicacies can also be enjoyed in izakaya bars, popular local bars where traditional Japanese snacks are prepared. The eyeballs are usually eaten informally, after a hard day's work.

There are a huge variety of recipes. Some chefs boil the eyes for hours in a tasty miso soup with soya and ginger until they completely fall apart and only the pupils and the hard lenses of the eyes remain. Other chefs fry them and serve them with rice, vegetables, and a spicy sauce.

Experts confirm that the eyeballs are an exquisite food and have enormous benefits but the true secret to their popularity is the price.

More tuna is eaten in Japan than anywhere else in the world, but the price of the meat is very high; so the eyeballs have become a surprisingly cheap alternative and a handy local delicacy.

JAPAN

Tokyo